Cryptocurrency

The Complete Beginner's Guide to Investing and Trading in Cryptocurrencies

© Copyright 2018 by John James - All rights reserved.

The following eBook is reproduced below, with the goal of providing information that is as accurate and reliable as possible. Regardless, purchasing this eBook can be seen as consent to the fact that both the publisher and the author of this book are in no way experts on the topics discussed within, and that any recommendations or suggestions that are made herein are for entertainment purposes only. Professionals should be consulted as needed prior to undertaking any of the actions endorsed herein.

This declaration is deemed fair and valid by both the American Bar Association and the Committee of Publishers Association and is legally binding throughout the United States.

Furthermore, the transmission, duplication or reproduction of any of the following work including specific information will be considered an illegal act, irrespective of if it is done electronically or in print. This extends to creating a secondary or tertiary copy of the work or a recorded copy and is only allowed with an express written consent of the Publisher. All additional rights reserved.

The information in the following pages are broadly considered to be a truthful and accurate account of facts, and as such any inattention, use or misuse of the information in question by the reader will render any resulting actions solely under their purview. There are no scenarios in which the publisher or the original author of this work can be in any fashion deemed liable for any hardship or damages that may befall them after undertaking information described herein.

Additionally, the information in the following pages is intended only for informational purposes and should thus be thought of as universal. As befitting its nature, it is presented without assurance regarding its prolonged validity or interim quality. Trademarks that are mentioned are done without written consent and can in no way be considered an endorsement from the trademark holder.

Table of Contents

Table of Contents 4

Introduction 6

Chapter 1: What Are Cryptocurrencies? 9
- What is A Cryptocurrency? 10
- But What are they, Really? 13
- Why Does Cryptocurrency Matter? 15
- Is There a Future in Cryptocurrency? 21
- Why Should I Invest in Cryptocurrency Now? 23

Chapter 2: Choosing A Cryptocurrency 26
- Bitcoin 27
- Ethereum 28
- Ripple 29
- Litecoin 30
- Monero 31
- Making an Investment Choice 33
- Making the Choice for Purchasing 34

Chapter 3: Buying and Storing Cryptocurrencies 36
- How Does Buying Work? 36
- Buying Your First Coins 38
- How Does Storing Work? 39
- Storing Your New Coins 42
- To Summarize 45

Chapter 4: Tips for Mastering Cryptocurrency Investing and Trading 49
   Buy with Funds You Don't Need............ 50
   Research First, Buy and Trade Second.. 52
   Diversify Only If You Understand 54
   Pay Attention to the Market Cap 55
   You Don't Have to Buy a Whole Coin 55
   Unless Circumstances Change, Don't Take Profits..57
   Cryptocurrency is Not for Day Traders . 59
   Buy Low, Sell High, And......................... 60
   Buy Now 61
   Buy the Rumor, Sell the News 63
   Practice and Get Comfortable 64

Conclusion 65

Introduction

Cryptocurrencies are the hottest craze in the financial world right now, with everyone wanting to learn more about them and find out how they can invest in these unique currency forms. The craze really sprung when Bitcoin was introduced in 2009 and soared over the years to the point where now, at the time of writing this, it is narrowing in on a value of $13,000 USD. With people realizing how incredible the returns can be on these investments, everyone is interested in finding how they can get their piece of the pie. The great thing is, this further increases the value of many of these currencies as the supply and demand balance leads more toward the demand than the supply.

If you have ever wondered how you can get involved in cryptocurrencies, then this book is perfect for you. "*Cryptocurrency*: The Complete Beginner's Guide to Investing and Trading in Cryptocurrencies" will answer any questions you might have about getting started in this lucrative investment opportunity. You will learn about exactly what a cryptocurrency is, how they came about, and what made them so popular. You will also learn about many of the most popular cryptocurrencies available on the market today and what makes them unique from other cryptocurrencies that are presently available. You will also learn about how to buy and sell, and store your cryptocurrencies. Finally, you will be given some of the best advice on how to truly get good at this investment practice so that you can make the most back from it.

Cryptocurrency investing can seem intimidating, especially if you are not overly familiar with the world of finances and cryptocurrencies themselves. However, it is actually extremely simple to get started and, with the right moves, you could end up earning incredible returns on your initial investments. The real key is in educating yourself and researching as much as possible so that you can make sound judgment calls and maximize your returns. You have come to the perfect place to acquire all of that information, too.

While this book will not go excessively into detail on each specific cryptocurrency available to you, it will help you get started and increase your confidence in this trading and investing strategy. You will also be guided towards how you can maximize your knowledge and increase your understanding so that you can make the most educated decisions on every investment you make.

If you are ready to begin tackling the world of cryptocurrency trading and investing, let's begin!

Chapter 1: What Are Cryptocurrencies?

When people think of cryptocurrency, most often the first thought in their mind is about Bitcoin. This popular cryptocurrency was the pioneer of digital currencies and has continued to dominate mainstream headlines everywhere. If you have already done some investigating into the world of cryptocurrencies, then you likely already know that there are many different currencies available to you nowadays. However, if this is your first time really digging deep, then you may be unaware that there are actually several different coins that you can use in addition to bitcoin in the modern cryptocurrency world.

Before we really get into the different kinds of cryptocurrency, however, why don't we take some time to understand what cryptocurrency actually is. This will give you the opportunity to have a clear understanding of what this type of currency is and why so many people are eager to invest in it. As well, when it comes to investing, you should always be clear on what it is exactly that you are investing in to prevent yourself from making a poor decision that results in you losing out on funds. So, before we get much further, let's explore what a cryptocurrency really is.

What is A Cryptocurrency?

Put simply, a cryptocurrency is a form of digital currency that is created, bought, sold, traded, and used all in the digital realm. There is no material object associated with the currency. Unlike traditional currencies which can be physically held through bills, coins, and other physical goods, cryptocurrencies are strictly dealt with on computers.

The concept for cryptocurrencies has been around for a long time. Back in the nineties, many different groups of people came together to try and design a cryptocurrency that would be successful and take away the need for traditional currencies. However, all of these attempts failed for one reason or another. In 2009, however, Bitcoin emerged. This cryptocurrency was the first successful one to ever hit the market, and even then it started out somewhat slow and with a great deal of concern and disbelief from the public. The creator, who goes by the alias Satoshi Nakamoto, was able to successfully design a coin that lived up to all of the initial desires and expectations of cryptocurrency. To this day, Bitcoin is still one of the most popular and widely traded cryptocurrencies. However, it is quickly finding itself amongst competition in recent years as new forms of cryptocurrencies are constantly emerging.

Cryptocurrency is built on a peer-to-peer network system. This means that there are no banks, financial institutions, or other third-parties involved with transactions that are conducted through cryptocurrencies. Instead, they are made through complex computer algorithms and then owned/traded by the owners themselves. There is no need to worry about banking fees, transaction fees, or any other fees as the currencies are not actually owned by anyone other than the holder of the currency itself.

Cryptocurrency is an incredible concept and is rapidly evolving into an incredible reality, too. This does not mean that it comes without faults, however. There are still many things that are being sorted out and understood by those who are responsible for creating the algorithms and facilitating the trades. For example, to facilitate payments and transactions, you need to use a payment network. One major problem that these networks used to face was the issue with double-spending. This is the practice of spending the same amount twice, and it can happen through loopholes in the system. Although this is an issue, it is not something that most people worry about. That is because, in modern cryptocurrencies, these networks use a decentralized system to keep records of balances. This means there are several servers responsible for keeping a record of transactions. If anyone were to try and alter the information within these servers to double-spend their cash, it would immediately be declined. No record of the attempted transaction would even be stored because it would be considered an illegitimate transaction and therefore it would simply be shut down.

This is the exact reason why cryptocurrencies failed for so long. Many of the developers were attempting to create a cryptocurrency that was based on a centralized server. This meant that a single server was responsible for the information stored around transactions. A simple hack into the system could result in the currency being double-spent as one could override the computer itself. However, Nakamoto managed to create and introduce a de-centralized server that created the same system we just discussed. As a result, the issue of double-spending is no longer a major issue with modern cryptocurrencies.

Upon realizing this, creating the de-centralized server system, and then launching Bitcoin, Nakamoto brought an entirely new era of possibility to cryptocurrencies. Now, all of the cryptocurrencies that have followed Bitcoin are built much in the same way, resulting in the process being far more secure for everyone involved.

But What are they, Really?

You now have a general idea of what cryptocurrencies are: a digital form of currency that can be used in place of traditional currencies. However, you may still be wondering about what they are *exactly*. As in, what exactly does a digital currency look like? How does it have any value? How does a server know that one even exists, to begin with? Let's look deeper into this so that you can understand the inner workings of cryptocurrencies and why they are a "thing" rather than just an illusion that someone made up.

Cryptocurrency

Like traditional currencies, cryptocurrencies have a basis. There is a "thing" in existence that proves there is a form of currency there, to begin with. Someone did not just wake up one day, decide to formulate an imaginary currency and begin exchanging a theory or an illusion. There is an actual physical representation of these currencies, even though it doesn't exist in a materialistic way. Just because you cannot hold the currency in your physical wallet or in your hand does not mean that there is not some form of proof of its existence. In fact, its existence is very real and valid. Here's how.

Essentially, at the very basis of what a cryptocurrency is, it consists of limited entries in a database that cannot be changed without specific conditions being fulfilled. This may not sound overly fancy or specific, but it does fully embody exactly what a cryptocurrency is.

If you want to get a really solid understanding of what the cryptocurrency world actually looks like, consider your online banking through your traditional bank. When you put funds into your account, the physical money you own is taken away and turned into a digital number on a screen. Then, every time you use your bank card to make a purchase, money is deducted from your account to reflect the new balance. If money is put into your account, you can see it added to your balance. Essentially, it is a database that manages your money, and the value cannot be changed without a certain condition being fulfilled. Those conditions would include spending it which would reduce your balance, or being given money which would increase it.

The same is true for cryptocurrency. There is a de-centralized database that recognizes these digital currency "entries." Each time you invest in or are paid in cryptocurrency, you are given a balance. If you spend it or sell it, your balance is reduced. At a very basic level, it is no different than using your bank balance on your debit card.

Why Does Cryptocurrency Matter?

The very fact that you are reading this book proves that cryptocurrency has sparked your interest. However, you may be wondering why people are so excited about it. What is so revolutionary about this new form of currency that people want to cultivate it and replace traditional currency with it? How can it truly be that different? The answer is simple: cryptocurrency is free of all of the limitations that are held by traditional currencies.

Cryptocurrency

The biggest reason why cryptocurrencies matter is based on the transactional properties held by the cryptocurrencies. These currencies have features that do not exist in traditional currency transactions which make them more secure, easier to access, and ultimately focused in a "for the people" approach. This is based on the peer-to-peer networking system that the currencies are built on. There are five primary transaction-based properties that make these currencies so revolutionary from traditional currencies. They are outlined in the following points.

Irreversible. When it comes to traditional currencies, particularly those held on a bank card or credit card, transactions can be reversed. This can be a major issue for retailers. In fact, this issue is fairly prominent and takes place on a daily basis. It is a scam whereby someone requests a service or purchases a product from a retailer. They pay with a debit or credit card. Then, later, they call their banking company and claim that the transaction was false and that they never made that transaction. The bank then reverses the transaction, refunding the individual with their funds. Now, they have received free products or services because the transaction was reversed. There is not a lot that a company can do when this happens, either, despite it being recognized as a form of fraud.

With cryptocurrencies, the transactions are irreversible. Once the de-centralized server is in agreeance with the transaction, and it has been processed, there is no way to remove its existence from the system. You cannot reverse it or otherwise commit fraud by having the transaction "removed." These transactions are also hard to manipulate or fraudulently put through as both the merchant and the customer require their own unique keychains or digital passwords to validate the transaction. After both parties have inputted their transactions, they have given permission for the transaction to be conducted and there is no way to claim otherwise. Since no one else has your key but you, there is no way for this to be fraudulently manipulated unless you intentionally give your key to someone else.

This also means, however, that if you send your money to a scammer or if somehow a hacker steals them from your computer that there is no way to reverse it and get your funds back. So, while it can protect merchants, it can also create an issue. There are a few security methods you can take to prevent this from happening, however. They include storing your funds in an offline wallet on your computer and validating every merchant or individual that you send funds to.

Pseudonymous. Your transactions and your accounts that hold your funds are not connected to your identity when it comes to cryptocurrencies. For that reason, no one can connect you to your specific transactions. Even though they can see that the transaction has taken place, they cannot identify that it was *you* who made it. They also cannot identify who the secondary person was in your transaction. The identities of those involved in the transactions are completely anonymous.

In modern transactions, identities are tied to all transactions. This means that banks and other individuals can monitor your transaction activities and see what you are doing. When it comes to a security feature, this is an incredibly valid and valuable feature to have. It is easy to quickly identify who the scammers are, who is committing fraud, and issue penalties where they belong, rather than the victim being forced to pay the price. However, it can also mean that individuals outside of authorities and law enforcement can see your transactions. While not everyone cares about this, some people may prefer to have their transactions kept private. For this reason, having your keys completely anonymous may be a benefit.

Fast and Global. When you conduct a transaction with cryptocurrency, the transaction is typically very fast. Depending on what payment network you are using, you can also request to pay a small fee to have your transaction moved into a higher-priority level so that it is processed even faster. This means that you can quickly transfer funds around, no matter how large they are. From a few dollars to a few hundred thousand dollars, you can send them with minimal effort. And, since the entire network is built on a global level, you can transact these currencies to virtually anywhere in the world with no fees outside of those which you choose to pay should you want to increase the priority level of your transaction. That means if you want to send hundreds of thousands of dollars across borders for a business transaction, it can be done so instantaneously and without paying any fees to convert currencies or send them across borders.

Cryptocurrency

This is an incredibly valuable feature as it means the cost of doing business becomes much more feasible for many, including startup companies. It also means that business can be conducted in a much shorter time frame as there are not several processes that need to be done and validated by banks before the transaction can be validated and considered "official" and complete.

Secure. Because of the decentralized system that cryptocurrencies are built on and the cryptography system used to create and transact them, cryptocurrencies are considered to be an incredibly secure form of currency. Short of you paying a scammer directly or someone hacking into your computer and stealing them, there are very few ways that your currencies can be fraudulently dealt with. It is virtually impossible to have people conduct fraudulent transactions with your currency, and once they are sent, they are gone. This means that there is no potential for the transaction to be interrupted, stolen, or otherwise affected or impacted in the transactional process.

Cryptocurrencies are built with personal keys, and these keys are extremely secure. It is nearly impossible for anyone to break into them and begin using your account against your permission. So, unlike a bank account which can be fraudulently hacked and then have funds stolen from it, your cryptocurrency account cannot be hacked. It is completely secure to you and your key.

Permissionless. One of the biggest things about currency in the traditional form is that you have to get your funds converted and that in some cases you need some form of permission to get your funds. Since governments control the funds, they can prevent and bar you from using or trading in their regional currency. Cryptocurrency is not like that, however. Instead, it is a software that can be downloaded for free. Then, you can immediately begin receiving and sending cryptocurrencies. There are no government or authority figures involved, so there are nothing and no one to prevent you from using the currency at your own free will.

Is There a Future in Cryptocurrency?

Based on the excitement and popularity around cryptocurrency, we can conclude that it is not going anywhere. At least not in the near future.

Cryptocurrency

Not only are people eager to purchase and use it as it is, but the idea of what cryptocurrency could mean for our future and how we live our lives is also incredible.

People speculate and dream that one day we will have a world whereby all of our devices and personal belongings are equipped with their own "keys" which can automatically perform payments for us. For example, if you are low on food you would tell your fridge to purchase more groceries for you based on a preset list you have chosen, and it would use cryptocurrency and its unique cryptocurrency key, which would be linked to your wallet, to complete the transaction. They also hope that this will be possible for cars when it comes to charging them, and other similar features.

In essence, cryptocurrency is believed to be a way for us to bring a futuristic sci-fi type of world into our reality sooner than any of us may have originally expected. Although all of these features could easily be done with traditional currencies, the idea that we could use cryptocurrencies and bypass all of the banks and be the sole dealers and accountants of our own funds is fascinating. Not only would they be globally recognized, therefore making banks and other traditional financial institutions obsolete, but they would also be free of any traditional fees that we presently recognize. This means that you would be able to effortlessly process transactions anywhere, at any time, with little to no restrictions.

If you wanted to transfer money to family in a different country, it would cost significantly less meaning they would get to keep more of the money. If you wanted to purchase something from overseas, the transaction would clear in record timing and allow for you to complete the purchase much quicker than is presently possible. If you wanted to run a global empire, your business could operate seamlessly with no need to worry about currency conversions and other traditional currency-related issues that sometimes pose a difficulty or time-consuming manner in the modern era.

Why Should I Invest in Cryptocurrency Now?

There are many reasons why people are already getting started in investing in cryptocurrencies even though we are not entirely sure of the role they will have in our world in the future. While we can speculate, there are no guarantees on what will or will not happen with these currencies. However, it has been concluded that they are here to stay and that one way or another they are going to have some form of impact on the world.

Currently, many people are purchasing cryptocurrencies as a means to hedge themselves against the ever-fluctuating value of their national currencies. As their own national currencies devalue, owning and trading in cryptocurrencies can be more productive. They tend to have a more stable value long-term, and they seem to be on the uptrend more often than not. Some have even reached as high as $12,000USD+ value per coin!

With the ever-rising value of these coins and the ever-fluctuating state of the economy, investing now is better than waiting too long. With how rapidly the technology around cryptocurrencies is evolving and developing, getting involved sooner rather than later is the best way to ensure that you get on board and maximize the income you earn as a result of your investments. Whether you want to purchase them now and hold onto them until they potentially become usable on a wide-scale, or if you want to purchase them and sell them in a trading strategy to increase your funds, they are a great asset to invest in. They can help you diversify your portfolio and effectively embrace the future as it rapidly speeds towards us in the present.

Chapter 2: Choosing A Cryptocurrency

There are many different types of cryptocurrencies that have sprung about since the release of Bitcoin in 2009. As a result, there has been a wide amount of speculation as to which currency is the best to invest in and where you should be putting your attention. Many of these coins are viable competitors to Bitcoin, with some even being considered better or more advanced in their abilities and potential. Others seem to exist on a much smaller scale and may or may not provide the same value or benefits that larger coins might.

When you get started in investing in cryptocurrency, you want to make sure that you are investing in the right currency. You want to make sure that you pick one that is going to suit what you are looking for in regards to investment purposes, as well as one that you can rely on and ideally earn a profit from if you are in the business of trading.

To help you learn more about each coin that is presently available, where it currently sits in the marketplace, and why you might consider investing in it, we are going to explore the most popular and well-known coins that have become available in the cryptocurrency market.

Bitcoin

Topping our list of currencies is Bitcoin. This coin is the most popular coin because of how famous it has become as a result of being a pioneer in the modern cryptocurrency world. It was the first to launch, and it has topped the charts ever since. Despite other coins coming out, Bitcoin has remained at the top of the popularity ranking since its launch in 2009. Despite its popularity, however, there are other cryptocurrencies that are rapidly encroaching on its territory in the way of them being valid competitors in the marketplace.

Bitcoin is said to be like a digital version of gold. It has been used globally for payment methods, and many different online and even offline merchants have begun accepting this currency as a form of payment for goods and services. When people discuss cryptocurrencies, Bitcoins are typically the first thing that comes to mind. These coins began at a value of $0 and were originally launched as a beta program. Developers wanted to try and see if they could find a valid cryptocurrency format that would work, and it's safe to say that they did. Not only is Bitcoin still in existence today and rapidly growing in popularity, with it rapidly approaching $13,000 USD in value, but also holds the title as the pioneer for modern cryptocurrency technology. It is safe to say that they certainly mastered the algorithm and successfully designed a cryptocurrency that is valid and useful when they launched Bitcoin!

Ethereum

Since its launch in 2015, Ethereum has rapidly become second-in-place for the best cryptocurrency to get involved in. Despite being second in the cryptocurrency hierarchy, however, Ethereum has an incredible addition that Bitcoin does not have. That is, Ethereum has been designed to not only perform basic transactions but also to perform complex contracts and programs. It does so by using the Blockchain technology that was introduced upon the creation of Bitcoin.

Ethereum smart contracts and programs are essentially complex contracts that are created to determine how and when money will be issued. Once certain conditions are met, money will be released to the appropriate party. If, however, these conditions are never met, the money is never released.

The interesting thing about Ethereum is that it is actually created to be more of a family or set of cryptocurrencies versus a single cryptocurrency like Bitcoin. This means that Ethereum hosts several "tokens" which are used as a currency form. Some include DigixDAO and Augur. These tokens are then used to complete payments and transfer funds. Each unique token carries a different value. It is quite similar to how you may carry coins in your own physical wallet. Some might be worth just $0.10 whereas others are worth $1 or $2. When you invest in Ethereum, it pays to invest in several different tokens to further diversify your portfolio and maximize your potential gains.

Ripple

It is important that we talk about Ripple despite it being considered one of the least popular cryptocurrencies on the market. You do not want to get involved with something without fully understanding it, and since Ripple is widely talked about, it is important that you are completely aware of what you are getting into if you begin exploring Ripple as a cryptocurrency investment option.

Ripple is a form of cryptocurrency that is less than a currency format and more of a debt format. The native cryptocurrency for this program is XRP, and it is not actually used as a medium to store and exchange value. Instead, it is used as a token to protect the network itself against spam.

Most people consider Ripple to be a poor investment and do not think it will last long or be worth it in the long run. Many cryptocurrency buffs call it a pre-mined software and believe it is not a real cryptocurrency but rather a network. However, the banks appear to really like Ripple and have begun adopting the system at an increasing pace.

Litecoin

Whereas Bitcoin is considered to be digital gold in the cryptocurrency world, Litecoin is considered to be digital silver. This coin quickly launched just after Bitcoin, making it the second cryptocurrency to truly emerge on the scene of modern cryptocurrencies.

When they developed Litecoin, it is believed that they developed it as a "2.0" version of Bitcoin. They made it so that the transactions and mining process are faster than in Bitcoin technology, and also so that there are more tokens, as well as new mining algorithms.

This cryptocurrency was perfectly designed to be the smaller and more readily available version of Bitcoin. Whereas Bitcoin may hold higher marketplace value and popularity, Litecoin tends to be much easier for people to get started with and use in investments and trading.

The biggest setback with Litecoin is that people preferred to use Bitcoin over Litecoin and therefore no one ever found a real use for it. For that reason, people stopped using it widely and instead favored Bitcoin. However, the coin is still mined and traded, and many people hoard it just in case Bitcoin ever fails.

Monero

After Bitcoin was created, developers realized there were further ways that security could be enhanced and the algorithms could be stronger. As a result, they developed the CryptoNight algorithm and launched Monero. The biggest example of how these two differ is with the blockchain transactions. Bitcoin is hashed on the blockchain, and a trail of transactions follows it, always. There is no way to cut through this. With Monero, however, you can cut through them.

The first time that the CryptoNight algorithm was introduced was in a coin known as Bytecoin, and it was highly rejected by the cryptocurrency community. This was because the cryptocurrency was heavily premined. However, they managed to later launch Monero which is the first time they ever launched the CryptoNight algorithm as a non-premined clone of the original Bytecoin. Although many others have since emerged, Monero has maintained its position as the most popular variation of a cryptocurrency existing with CryptoNight algorithms.

Monero has continued to steadily increase in pricing, however the ways it can be used remains extremely small. For that reason, it may be worth investing in, but many people are losing faith that it will have any form of significant future in the economy or marketplace. Rather than being a good investment as a currency itself, the technology is a better investment as it provides a form of playground for the developers to build on.

Making an Investment Choice

Choosing which coin to invest in really depends on what you are looking for. If you want to have a basic coin that you can invest in and trade, Bitcoin is likely the best way for you to go. This cryptocurrency revolves around a single form of token and is the most popular, which is likely the very reason why the price has continued to steadily increase for nearly a decade since the technology was launched.

The next best form of currency to get into is Ethereum. This currency is rapidly sidling up to Bitcoin as the best cryptocurrency technology and easily takes second place as most popular. While Ethereum is more of a family of tokens versus a single kind, it is still a great cryptocurrency to invest in. If you choose to invest in Ethereum, make sure you choose one of the more popular token to invest in, such as the DigixDAO or Augur. Do your research before investing in any particular token so that you are not investing in something that will not earn you a strong return.

If you want to consider a less-expensive and still fairly valuable coin to invest in, Litecoin is a great place to start. While you will not make nearly as much return as you will with Bitcoin or Ethereum, it is a much lower buy-in and can be a great way to diversify your cryptocurrency investment profile and also protect yourself should Bitcoin ever fail.

If you are considering investing in something different that is considered to be more of a playground or a test program, Monero may be the way to go. While you likely will not get a strong return on this coin, you will be on the trail of a new form of an algorithm that has emerged in the cryptocurrency world. This means that if anything ever changes and goes strongly in Monero's favor, you will already be on board.

Avoid investing in Ripple at all costs. There is very little to be said about this program other than the fact that it is not widely accepted, not an advancement on technology, and will likely not go anywhere. You will not make a strong return on your investment and will likely find yourself out a lot of money if you trail this cryptocurrency and try to earn any form of return on it.

Making the Choice for Purchasing

If you are looking to get into a currency that you can both invest in and purchase products with, Bitcoin and Ethereum remain the two best choices. Both of these have a wide and ever-growing range of uses and are being accepted by more and more merchants all of the time. Not only are you likely to make a great return on your investment, but you can also actively use them for shopping and transactions to get an idea of what purchasing things with cryptocurrency is truly like.

The other forms of cryptocurrency have a very small backing in the marketplace which means that there are few things you can actually purchase with them. While they may be okay for trading and investing, or diversifying your investments portfolio, they are not ideal when it comes to shopping of any sort.

Chapter 3: Buying and Storing Cryptocurrencies

After you have chosen the type of cryptocurrency or cryptocurrencies you want to begin investing in, you can go ahead and start the process of buying and storing them. In this chapter, we will discuss how these two parts of the process work and what you need to do to get started yourself.

How Does Buying Work?

Buying cryptocurrencies can be fun and easy and has the potential to help you earn a great return if you get involved in it in regards to trading. However, you have to first know how to actually buy your tokens or coins before you can begin doing anything with them.

Buying any cryptocurrencies is different from getting other forms of currency. You are not simply compensated for something and then head to the bank to cash in or switch it to a different currency if you want to make money through another means. Instead, you have to use digital platforms to buy your coins.

There are many platforms available for purchasing cryptocurrencies on. In general, they work fairly simply: find a platform, create an account, and begin. However, you need to make sure that you are using the best platform to get started. Some platforms are less secure, go offline frequently, or may not have access to the types of coins you want to invest in. So, be sure to research the specific platform that you want to use before you get started. A great place to start if you are looking to trade in any of the cryptocurrencies mentioned in the previous chapter of this book is Coinbase. In the next section where we talk about buying your first tokens, we will talk about Coinbase specifically.

Using a more well-known and popular purchasing platform means that you have more secured transactions and that the platform remains online more. Some may go offline regularly which can make buying and trading in cryptocurrencies annoying and frustrating. There are also a lot less glitches and kinks with more well-known applications.

Once you have chosen an application, it is as simple as making an account and getting started. On your platform, you will see that you have the opportunity to purchase and sell your coins. You will find more information and tips regarding what to do in the buying and selling process in Chapter 4, but ultimately that is the gist of it. It truly is one of the simplest investments to get started on. The biggest part of the process is research, the investment process itself takes minimal timing.

Buying Your First Coins

Now that you know how easy it is to get started, it's time to learn how you can buy your first tokens! As previously mentioned, this process is outlined using the Coinbase application or network, which is currently the most widely used one. However, any network you choose to use will work in the same general manner.

With Coinbase, you want to start by either downloading the application on your phone or visiting the Coinbase website. There, you will find a "sign up" button that allows you to begin creating your account. You will need to input some basic personal information, including your name, e-mail and chosen password. Then, you will need to go ahead and confirm that you agree to the terms and conditions of the website. Once you have done so, they will e-mail you a verification e-mail. You will need to open that e-mail and click the link to confirm your account.

With your account completely verified and ready to go, it is time to start buying coins! This part of the process is extremely simple. Go to either the application or website and login with your new account information. Then, add a way to purchase. This is typically by linking your bank account to the application. Once you have, you can simply tap the "Buy" button on the app, or the "Buy/Sell" tab on the website. Hit the buy button once more and then determine which type of currency you want to buy and how much US dollars you want to spend to purchase that currency. Next, it will tell you how much of the currency you are buying. Confirm the transaction, and you are done!

There are other cryptocurrency exchanges that are up-and-coming and popular among the cryptocurrency world. If you are looking for the opportunity to begin purchasing and selling and do not want to use Coinbase, other contenders include Kraken, Poloniex, Bittrex, Binance, Bitfinex, Bithumb, Shapeshift, Kucoin, Cobinhood, Coinone, CEX.IO, and Coinsquare.io.

How Does Storing Work?

Storing your cryptocurrencies requires you to have a cryptocurrency wallet. It is imperative that you store your coins properly to prevent yourself from losing them or having them stolen. While many networks, such as Coinbase, will provide you with a wallet, keeping them somewhere slightly more secure is a good idea.

When it comes to storing cryptocurrencies, there are two types of wallets. They are hot wallets and cold wallets. A hot wallet is stored online and is subjected to more risks and potential threats than a cold wallet, which is stored offline. Cold wallets are not connected to the internet which makes them a lot harder for anyone to hack into and steal your funds. If you are going to be storing or trading fairly large amounts, it is a good idea to store the bulk of your funds in a cold wallet and only store what you are actively going to use in a hot wallet.

Your wallet has a private key, and it is mandatory that you give this key to *no one*, not even your spouse or anyone that you trust. This means that you should also refrain from using wallets that are based on major exchange networks because the keys are stored on their servers which can make them easier to access if someone were to hack the servers. Ideally, this would never happen, but you can never be to safe when your funds are involved! To really ensure that you protect yourself, you want to make sure that you always store the bulk of your funds in a cold wallet, as previously mentioned. Only store them in a hot wallet if you are actively trading or using them. That way if your hot wallet ever gets hacked, the substantial portion of your funds are protected offline.

Hot wallets are available by downloading applications or using computer websites that work to store cryptocurrencies. Some of the most popular ones include Coinbase (only what you are going to be exchanging right away or in the very near future), Blockchain.info, Electrum, and Ledger or Trezor.

Cold wallets work differently. They require you to do what is called a paper wallet, where you essentially download a document that contains all of the information you need to generate the private keys that you need to access your coins. Generally, this exists on a piece of paper that has a QR code that you can scan into a software wallet when you want to access them. When you store your cryptocurrencies offline like this, it makes them significantly safer against hacking and fraud. However, you can also store them offline on a USB drive or other external media, on a bearer item such as those known as "physical bitcoins," or even on an offline hardware wallet available for cryptocurrency traders.

This may seem confusing, but once you get the hang of it, it becomes easier for you to understand. In the following section, we will discuss exactly how you can store your coins.

Storing Your New Coins

There are two methods of storage we are going to discuss: hot wallets and cold wallets. As previously mentioned, you want to store the majority of, if not all of, your coins in your cold wallet. The only coins you need to save in your hot wallet are those that you plan on using or trading in the near future. We are going to start by discussing your hot wallet as this is where your newly purchased coins will be transferred into.

If you are using Coinbase, you will have your coins automatically transferred into your Coinbase wallet. However, you may choose to use an alternative wallet or create a new wallet if you are using a different exchange. The easiest way to generate an online wallet is to go to Bitcoin.org if you are choosing to exchange in Bitcoin, and Jaxx or Electrum. These are software-based wallets that are considered hot wallets because they store your coins online on a mobile platform. To create a wallet with these platforms, simply visit their websites and follow the steps to create your own wallet. They will outline them for you, making the process extremely simple.

Now, when it comes to doing a cold wallet, it takes a bit longer. This depends on what type of cold wallet you intend on creating. Below we have outlined the steps for making a paper wallet. These are the easiest form of offline wallets you can create that will protect your investment and keep your funds safe. As long as you do not lose the paper, you are completely fine. You should store the paper in a safe place where it will not become damaged, and then you can easily access your funds at any time that you need them. This guide is for Bitcoin, but you can do the same for any cryptocurrency by accessing the native website and following similar steps. Here's how.

First, you want to go to the Bitcoin.com website and access the paper wallet tool. There, you want to press Ctrl-S to save the page locally to your computer. You also want to make sure that you create an offline address when you are there. Then, close out of the webpage and disconnect your computer from the internet.

Cryptocurrency

This will only be for a few minutes until you are done creating your paper wallet, then you can reconnect it.

After it is disconnected, open the save file of the website you just saved locally. Once you have, you want to move your mouse around and then tap some random keys on your keyboard a few times. This causes it to create a random Bitcoin address that will be equipped with both a public and private key-pair. This address will have been created completely offline since you disconnected from the internet when you were creating it.

Once you have created your key, print the page. You want to do this while the computer is still disconnected from the internet. To print the page, you want to make sure that your printer is also offline and manually connected to your computer. You do not want to have any of your devices connected to the internet during this process as this can compromise your key-pair.

With your page now printed in this manner, you have a completely offline set of public and private keys that are not documented online. The page you have will be equipped with a QR code for your private key and a visible copy of your public key. Keep this somewhere secure, such as in a fireproof safe to prevent it from becoming damaged or destroyed under any circumstances.

Once you have completely printed this off and you are done, you can reconnect your device to the internet and begin using your computer as normal once more. Never share your private key with anyone, regardless of this is online or offline. Sharing it could result in you losing your funds which would be devastating and disappointing.

If you want to add money to this wallet, you simply want to scan the public QR code and place it into the exchange where you would be "sending funds." This can be done on any popular cryptocurrency exchange network.

To redeem the coins, simply use a hot wallet that supports private keys and scan the QR code or use the private key address. Then, you will be able to access and redeem any of the funds you have in the wallet.

To Summarize

Getting started with cryptocurrency trading is not as hard as it may sound. In fact, it is pretty simple once you understand it. The biggest key is determining which currency you want to invest in, and then learning how you can purchase, spend, and store your coins. It is important that you use a trusted network when purchasing and selling your coins to refrain from being scammed. Even though the network itself is typically safe, there are many instances where untrustworthy people may get involved in deals with you and then take your coins without returning funds as promised. As well, even though it's not common on the major exchange networks, they can be hacked which can compromise your private information. It is important that you choose one that is verified as safe and that is not known to have any fraudulent activity taking place on it at any given time. You can easily do some online research about the network you want to use before you commit to ensure that you are using a safe one that will not result in you having any negative experiences with your investing and trading.

Once you have opened your account, buying is extremely simple. Most of the major exchange networks will walk you through the process step-by-step. They also have built-in wallets. They will also guide you toward other recommended wallets to store your cash. Remember, these are called hot wallets for a reason. That is because they are somewhat unsafe. You should never store a large amount of your coins in these wallets. Instead, store them safely in an offline manner such as with a paper wallet. Then, when you need to access them, transfer them to your hot wallet. The only coins you should have access to from your hot wallet are ones that you are going to use in the immediate or very near future. If there is going to be any gap of time between when you receive them and when you plan on using them, you should move them to your cold wallet. It only takes a few minutes, and it can truly save you from having a potentially devastating experience of losing your coins to some form of fraudulent activity, such as a hack. Even hot wallets that are considered to be the most secure are not completely free of risk, so you want to do your best to protect your investment and be smart about your storage solutions.

Once you have stored your funds, you can easily transfer them back into your hot wallet to be used at any time. Simply put them into the hot wallet and sell them to receive your native or desired currency, or you can spend them with merchants who accept the form of cryptocurrency that you have available to shop with.

Cryptocurrency

It may seem extremely confusing at first, especially when you first see all of the screens associated with the exchanges, trading, hot wallets, and cold wallets. However, once you get the hang of it by trying it out a time or two, it becomes significantly easier. Soon, you will be buying, selling, trading, and spending cryptocurrencies as effortlessly as you presently do with your traditional currency.

Chapter 4: Tips for Mastering Cryptocurrency Investing and Trading

To make sure you get the most of your experience and truly master the art of trading with cryptocurrency, we are going to discuss some tips that you can use to master the art of cryptocurrency investing and trading. Using these tips will ensure that you do not make any fatal beginner mistakes and that you protect your assets and maximize the returns you get from your investments.

It is a good idea to review these tips *before* you begin investing to ensure that you know as much as you can before you get started. Although it is a fairly simple concept and you can get started relatively easily, it is important that you know as much as you can before you invest any of your cash into these currencies. If you do it right, you are likely to make a great return. Plus, it is always proper investment etiquette to make sure that you effectively research any investment before you actually invest in it. That way you don't make any uneducated decisions that could result in you losing out on cash!

Buy with Funds You Don't Need

Especially when you are getting started, you should only invest with funds that you do not need. If you think you may be able to invest in a cryptocurrency with money that you actually need so that you can double it and get-rich-quick, think again. Investments, especially in cryptocurrencies, are something that takes time to accumulate and build money. While you may get lucky and make a couple of hundred dollars, or even a couple of thousand dollars, in a relatively short period of time, you should not expect that this will happen. Generally, when you invest in cryptocurrencies, you should expect your investment to stay put for a fairly lengthy amount of time. The longer you leave your investment, the better your return on it will be. For that reason, you only want to use money that you don't need.

In addition to giving you a greater chance to earn more, it also saves you from a potential financial ruin if you invest money that you didn't have to begin with. If you were to invest it and something went wrong in your investment, and you lost all of your funds, or if the market crashed and the value of the currency went out the window, you want to make sure that you didn't have a lot riding on that investment. A general rule of thumb when investing in something as volatile and unpredictable as cryptocurrency is that you never want to invest with money that you expect you will need. Instead, invest and hope for the best, but prepare for the worst. If you come out on top with a healthy return on your investment, that's great! Ideal, even. However, if you end up coming out on the bottom, you want to be sure that the money you had tied up in your investments wasn't essential to your overall wellbeing. This is not only true with cryptocurrency investments but any investment in general.

A good way to start is to take a small amount of money and invest it. Many people like to start with just $50-$100. Then, they invest it and play around with it to see how it works. Learn what to watch for in the marketplace, how to buy, and when to sell. Once you get the hang of it with a smaller amount, you can begin putting more and more funds into it whenever you desire. You may choose to put a set amount each check into the investment, or you may simply put extra funds in any time you have them. Either way, make sure it's extra money and not money you need. Even if you seem to have "mastered" it, you should know that there is always a chance that it could go south, fast.

This is not to scare you from investing at all, only to warn you against investing poorly.

Research First, Buy and Trade Second

It is imperative that you research cryptocurrency before you buy into it. You are off to a great start by reading this book. Now, you have a strong idea of what the most popular forms of cryptocurrency are, how you can acquire them, how you can store them, and how you can trade or use them. That is important. However, you should not let it stop here.

When you are investing in anything, including cryptocurrencies, it is important that you invest in them *after* you have researched them. You do not want to find yourself investing in something that you don't fully understand, only to lose your investment because you were not clear on what you were doing. It is important that you spend time researching the exchange network you are going to use, the cryptocurrency form that you want to invest in, and the recent and historical market figures for that particular coin.

A great way to research cryptocurrency comes from basic internet searches, but you should go deeper than that, too, if you want to make a really informed decision. There are many cryptocurrency forums and groups online that you can get into that will connect you with people who have already been trading in cryptocurrencies for quite some time. Getting involved in these forums gives you the opportunity to communicate with other traders and find out what is the best move for you to make at your beginner stage. The market is constantly changing, and so are the available currencies. For this reason, anything we may be able to recommend to you right now in this book may quickly become invalid. That is why we have not recommended any one specific coin for you to get started with but rather educated you on the most popular coins at the time of writing this book.

In addition to researching before you trade the first time, make sure you continue to research before every major trade and throughout the duration of your investments. As we just discussed, the market is constantly changing, and so are the range of available cryptocurrencies. It could change at any given time with the introduction of a new technology or cryptocurrency, so you want to make sure that you stay on top of it and pay attention. The more you research first, the more likely you will make wise, educated investment decisions. This can protect you against uneducated decisions that could cost you in the long run, and helps you get more out of your investments.

Diversify Only If You Understand

To expand on the importance of researching first, make sure that you only diversify when you understand what you are diversifying for, and what you are diversifying into. Some people suggest that you buy a small amount of every cryptocurrency currently available. This is actually a really poor investment choice. Some you can already clearly tell are not going to be very much, and if you were to do some research, you would know that. Some are simply experiments to learn about new technology and see what can be done with cryptocurrency. Others are revealed as an opportunity for new developers to get in on the cryptocurrency buzz and are not actually developed that well at all, making them virtually useless to you. There is no sense wasting any of your funds in these types of cryptocurrencies when you could simply research them and invest in ones that are more likely to succeed.

Furthermore, do not look to diversify your portfolio right away. Start with one cryptocurrency that you have already researched and spend some time getting to know how to use the cryptocurrency, how to navigate the exchange, and how to use your wallet storages. Once you have gotten comfortable with that cryptocurrency, look at alternative solutions of what you can buy into, and then buy into them once you are ready. Never buy into a currency that you don't understand, or into a wide series of cryptocurrencies without any clear understanding of why you are investing in them. You don't want to waste any of your assets investing in things that are going nowhere. You can find this out simply by researching them. Always research first, buy second. This includes when it comes to diversifying out into alternative coins.

Pay Attention to the Market Cap

You Don't Have to Buy a Whole Coin

Many people falsely believe that if you cannot afford to buy an entire coin, there is no sense getting involved in the market. That is completely false. If you want to get into Bitcoin or any other expensive cryptocurrency, you can do so with whatever funds you have available to you. This may seem confusing, especially since with traditional currency we couldn't possibly dream of owning a portion of a coin and it being worth anything, but in cryptocurrency terms, it makes complete sense.

When you own a percentage of a coin, then realistically other people would combine to own the other percentage of the same coin. When you choose to sell your percentage, you will make back that percentage of the coin.

To make it sound less confusing, let's look at a basic example.

Say a coin is worth $1,000 and you invest $100 in the coin. You then own 10% of that coin. If the coin value increases to $10,000, then your 10% of the share would increase to $1,000. Because it is a digital asset, you can easily own a share of a coin, versus the entire coin itself. Do not feel as though you cannot invest in a coin simply because you do not currently have the market value of the coin. For example, when bitcoin reaches $13,000, you do not need $13,000 to buy the coin. Instead, buy a portion of it with the funds you do have.

Cryptocurrency exchanges allow you to choose how much of your native currency you want to invest in the coin, and then they give you that respective percentage of the coin. Even if you only own 0.002% of the coin, which is a considerably small portion it seems, you can still make a significant return if the market goes up 20%.

Do not worry about how much of the coin you can buy, simply worry about investing in the one that suits your needs. If you want to invest $50 in a $13,000 coin, you can still make a fair return on that. There is nothing that states that you cannot do this. Do not be afraid of this number; you can still safely invest in these coins in most cases.

Unless Circumstances Change, Don't Take Profits

Many people feel that you should take the profits of your funds out right away. Of course, this is entirely up to you. Most people will say that you should go ahead and quickly sell so that you can collect a massive profit. If that is what works for you and that is what you are looking for, then, by all means, do that.

However, ideally, there are only a few things that would result in you really needing to remove your funds. For example, if your income changes and you really need the funds, you could sell them and take your profits. Or, if you choose that you want to remove your funds and invest elsewhere. You may also choose to remove your initial investment for peace of mind so that you know for sure that no matter what happens, you are not going to lose your original investment.

Of course, you may have other personal reasons for wanting to remove your profits that may be entirely up to you. If you really need them, if you want to go on a vacation, or really anything else. It *is* your funds, so it is entirely up to you what you choose to do with them. However, it is worth noting that the longer they sit, the bigger they grow. Rather than dipping into them, unless absolutely necessary, it may be a better idea to leave them alone and let them continue to accumulate so that one day when you do actually need them, they are available to you.

Cryptocurrency is Not for Day Traders

Many modern traders have a tendency to skim the market on a daily basis. They enter in the morning with low buy-ins and sell in the evening with high payouts. This is completely fine in many market places, but it is not a valuable practice in cryptocurrency. When it comes to cryptocurrency, you want to let it sit and accumulate for as long as possible. Rapidly buying and selling your funds can result in you losing out on valuable growth.

If you want to invest in cryptocurrency, you should look to it as a long-term investment instead of something that you can get in and out of in a relatively short period of time. While some people choose to take the profits and make massive returns in a short period of time, the real prize is in letting it sit and accumulate. The longer it sits, the bigger it grows. It is not unheard of for people to buy in with $1,000 and walk out with $80,000.

For this same reason, do not worry about being right on every single trade. You are going to make mistakes that will result in you not getting the maximum return on your investment. This is especially the case if you are new and if you do not have any substantial experience with investments. Instead of trying to be right every single time and making minimal investments, seek to be right when it really counts and make the most of your investments that you can. The goal is to make as much money as possible, so seek to do that and don't worry about mistakes you make along the way. You will learn and do better for the most part. But also, not every mistake can be completely avoided. Even the most advanced and avid traders in virtually every market make massive mistakes on a fairly consistent basis. A good trader, however, will know how to make decisions following that which will bring them back into the green.

Buy Low, Sell High, And…

When it comes to buying low and selling high, this is virtually always true in no matter what market you are trading in. So, naturally, it counts for cryptocurrencies as well. Because of how volatile the cryptocurrency market can be, however, this may not always be easy. It is hard to predict where the peaks and valleys are going to lie with cryptocurrencies as they can often take massive and seemingly irrational turns one way or another at any given time.

Instead of worrying so much about buying low and selling high, focus on buying low, holding onto the coins as long as you can, and then selling when they're high. You may not be able to predict the peaks due to the volatility of the market, so you want to make sure that you are focused on the long-term gains, not the short-term ones. Trying to predict the market in a short period of time can get stressful and result in you losing out on potentially major gains. Instead, look at the bigger picture and pay attention to it overall. Look beyond 24-hour spans and into weeks, or even months and years. This makes it much easier to determine where the general market is going and what moves you should make as a result.

Buy Now

Many people are worried about when to buy into the market. They are unsure about when they should buy in, they don't know if it is the right time, and they want to make sure that they get the most back. This is completely normal and natural. Obviously, this is likely why you are investing in cryptocurrency: to make a return. However, there is no optimal buy-in time. The longer you wait, the higher the price goes, and the higher your buy-in price will be.

Do not wait for the right time or try and predict when a valley will come so that you can buy in. Instead, buy in right now. Buy only what you can afford, get started with that, and then focus on buying *more* once it hits a low point. That makes it much easier for you to actually get started and not feel quite so intimidated in the world of cryptocurrency. For the first week or two, make it about learning and getting used to the market. Then, once you have, you can start paying attention to pulling the right moves and getting your low buy-ins and high payouts.

The only really bad move you can make when it comes to buying into a cryptocurrency is waiting so long that you become intimidated by the idea, or not completely researching the currency you choose to buy into before you actually buy into it. Take enough time to research, and then pull the trigger. If you start with a relatively small amount, like $100 or less, then it won't hurt so much if you make mistakes in the learning process. Keeping the pressure off in the beginning while you learn to understand it can make the entire process a lot easier.

Buy the Rumor, Sell the News

There is a phrase in trading that goes "buy the rumor, sell the news." This essentially means that you want to listen to what rumors are saying and, if many are in agreeance, buy in. For example, if there are rumors that a certain coin is going to rapidly increase in value, buy in! Then, if and when it actually does increase, you will be the one selling the news, not reading it or listening to it.

Although this can sometimes result in you not always making the best trades or losing out, it also puts you in the running to stand for a lot of gains. Since the entire idea is to earn as many funds as you possibly can, the more you stand to win, the better. Of course, you do not want to make an uneducated decision, so make sure that the rumors you are listening to are coming from reputable sources. Pay attention to other traders, media surrounding trades and investments, and other similar sources. As long as the rumor comes from a credible source and there are many people spreading the rumor, there is a good chance that it could come true. If you are worried about it not coming true, however, you can always invest a smaller amount.

Practice and Get Comfortable

The ultimate goal when it comes to trading and investing in cryptocurrencies is that you take your time, practice, and get comfortable. If you practice with funds that were not necessary and that you won't be overly upset over if you lose them, then any mistakes you make early on will not be as upsetting.

Getting started in anything new, especially trades and investments, can be confusing. Early on, you are learning to navigate new software, store your coins, and understand the market. Give yourself some time and some practice money to figure it all out, and then once it begins to make sense to you, you can start investing more into it. The more you learn to navigate the software, get used to transferring your funds and storing them, and knowing when to buy and when to sell your coins, the easier it becomes. As well, this will give you time to learn how to be patient and accumulate overall market gains, rather than getting antsy and buying and selling too frequently. Once you get used to the entire process, it will be easy for you and you will likely find that you can create incredible returns with this form of investment and trading.

Conclusion

Cryptocurrency is the way of the future, there is no doubt about it. Whether it is only going to be an addition to the existing currency, or if it will eventually replace it entirely, it pays to get on board and begin learning how cryptocurrencies work. Furthermore, there can be some pretty substantial profits made from investing in cryptocurrencies.

Getting started can be intimidating, especially if you have never been directly involved in investments or trades before. Unlike traditional currency whereby you can hire an investment portfolio manager to do the work for you, you are responsible for investing in and trading your own cryptocurrencies. Fortunately, there are many exchange networks you can use that make this process easy, even for beginners who have very little background knowledge on the trading side of finances.

I hope this book was able to help you understand more about how cryptocurrencies work, why they are so revolutionary, and what you need to do to begin trading them. Remember, this book is a beginner's guide, and it gives you phenomenal information to get started and actively buy, use, trade, and store cryptocurrencies. However, before you fully commit to any particular cryptocurrency, it is important that you take additional time to research that specific cryptocurrency. There are constantly new forms of cryptocurrencies emerging, and each one has unique traits, properties, and benefits. They also change rapidly, and so too can their popularity. If you want to make the best move, it is a good idea to investigate the specific coin you are most interested in before you commit to purchasing anything.

The next step is for you to determine which cryptocurrency best encompasses what you want to gain from cryptocurrency, and research it further. Then, when you are ready, you can create an account with a popular exchange network and create your hot wallet. Once everything is set up, you can go ahead and begin purchasing, selling, and trading currencies. Be sure that you start small so that any mistakes you may make early on as you are learning are not devastating to your overall finances. Only use funds that you do not need for any other reason.

Lastly, if you enjoyed this book, please take the time to honestly review it on Amazon Kindle. Your honest feedback would be greatly appreciated.

John James

Thank you, and good luck!

www.ingramcontent.com/pod-product-compliance
Lightning Source LLC
Chambersburg PA
CBHW030047230526
45471CB00003B/977